Words of Songs

Chenelle V Stancle

Words of Songs

© 2021 Chenelle V Stancle

Presentation by *BookLeaf Publishing*

Web: www.bookleafpub.com

E-mail: info@bookleafpub.com

ISBN: 9789358360264

First edition 2021

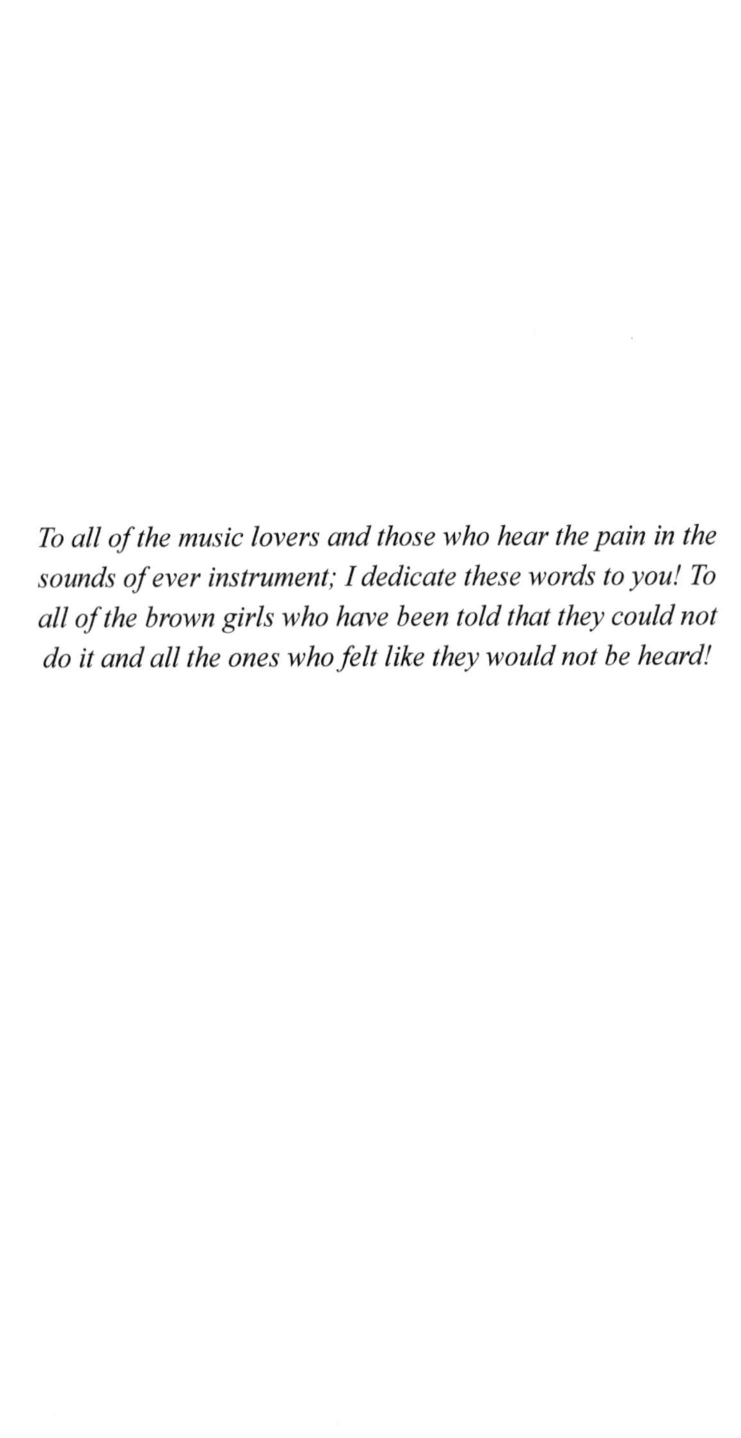

To all of the music lovers and those who hear the pain in the sounds of ever instrument; I dedicate these words to you! To all of the brown girls who have been told that they could not do it and all the ones who felt like they would not be heard!

Acknowledgement

To God who gave me this gift, I thank you! To my mom who set the tone for my life with all of the book subscriptions when I was a child. To my Soul Sista Monique, thank you for believing in me, encouraging me, and pushing me to keep going! To my cousin who continuously says, "Girl write that book." To anyone I've ever written something for, to everyone who has ever believed in me, and to me for getting out of my own way!

Preface

Words are more powerful than anyone could ever imagine. It has never taken many words to get ones point across. Poems are used to express the deepest feelings that may otherwise never be shared.

1. How does it Feel?

The sweetest thing I'd never know was the love you'd never show.

2. Mona Lisa

What is healing?

Is it the act of feeling?

Is it not feeling?

Is it self-destruction?

Breaking down parts put together at production.

Or is it like a puzzle?

Piece by Piece coming together.

It's all that and more.

Inclusive of all that you were before.

The creation of a masterpiece.

3.   Instrumental

The most piercing rhythm I ever felt was the sound of my own heartbreaking.

4. Lost One

The most painful truth is knowing you won't and can't always have the person you love.

5. Where Do I Fit In?

Seeking peace,

Needing rest!

I wonder what's the purpose of this test.

Where do I go?

Who's there to help?

 Lord please guide me and show me my next step.

5. Break Every Chain

Seeking solace to replace the pain, knowing that peace is the future gain.

7. One of them days

Feel like I want to cry, not even sure why

But the sun will come, and the tears will dry

And my light will shine when the moon is high

8. Steady Love

A jack of all trades, A man of many ways

 A shoulder to lean on, A supporter to welcome me home.

A lover like no other, A brotha'

A man that makes me feel safe, A man that deals in grace

A man that ends the chase, A man that gives himself away

A love that stays the same. Feelings that never change

9. All My Love

Even when it hurts, I'll be there to hold you. Even when it hurts, I'll be there to console you. Even when it hurts me, I'll be there to love you. So, call me when it hurts.

10. Before I let Go

Holding on as tight as I can,

I'm losing my grip

but I'm learning to stand!

So, take my hand and be my man

Or let go as slow as you can!

11. Say Goodbye

If I don't leave, you never will!

12. Pick Up Your Feelings

Am I allowed to quit? No!

Am I allowed to sit? No!

I'm allowed to grab my things, tuck them away, and make it through the day!

13. Understanding

Tell me so that I will know, or I will assume, and things will end soon.

14. Ready is Always Too Late

Same page, different stage, old ways, Feelings change.

15. I wish I wasn't

Loving you is detrimental to my spirit but losing you would be detrimental to my soul.

16. Superpower

He was my kryptonite, and he used that to ignite the flame in me that burned endlessly!

17. Always Will

No matter the distance

the time of the day

I'll always be willing, to stay!

18. Fire We Make

Every time I see you, I get this feeling in the pit of
my stomach. Even the sight of your name drives
me insane. It's something different. It's something
new. Please tell me, who am I without you?

19. Never Too Much!

I could devour every inch of you and still want more.

20. You are the Reason

My dedication,

My inspiration,

My heart's location,

I feel free,

No longer afraid to be the gentle me,

It's because of you,

My Muse!

www.ingramcontent.com/pod-product-compliance
Lightning Source LLC
LaVergne TN
LVHW010256210726
843508LV00020B/2794